SANDWICHES WITHOUT BREAD

100 Low-Carb, Gluten-Free Options!

Daria Polukarova

Skyhorse Publishing

Skyhorse Publishing books may be purchased in bulk at special discounts for sales promotion, corporate gifts, fund-raising, or educational purposes. Special editions can also be created to specifications. For details, contact the Special Sales Department, Skyhorse Publishing, 307 West 36th Street, 11th Floor, New York, NY 10018 or info@skyhorsepublishing.com.

Skyhorse® and Skyhorse Publishing® are registered trademarks of Skyhorse Publishing, Inc.®, a Delaware corporation.

Visit our website at www.skyhorsepublishing.com.

10 9 8 7 6 5 4 3 2 1

Library of Congress Cataloging-in-Publication Data is available on file.

Cover design by Mona Lin
Cover photograph by Daria Polukarova

Print ISBN: 978-1-5107-3236-0
Ebook ISBN: 978-1-5107-3238-4

Printed in China

SANDWICHES WITHOUT BREAD

Table of Contents

Introduction

Grabbing a sandwich often seems like the quickest, cheapest, and the most convenient lunch option. But if you are paleo, gluten-free, or just someone who is trying to cut some carbs out of your diet, things can get tricky.

The easiest alternative can be one of those expensive gluten-free breads . . . or, another option is making your own sandwich base from scratch. Take a look at the products you usually use as a sandwich filling—fresh lettuce and other greens, vegetables, eggs, meat or bean patties, etc. All of these can replace regular white bread, rolls, buns, and baguettes, and once you start experimenting, the options are endless!

Removing (or at least cutting down on) regular bread from your diet will not only help you reduce the amount of consumed simple carbohydrates, but it will also give you an opportunity to exponentially increase health benefits for your body on a daily basis. These benefits can include: increasing your intake of cellulose and complex carbohydrates, improving your blood glucose levels, improving memory and clarity of thinking, and higher energy levels, to name a few. Plus, the unique options offered here are so addictive, you'll want to try a new one every week!

This book will show you how to take your breadless sandwiches to the next level, using ingredients you're likely quite familiar with already.

Important Dietary Notes

All of the recipes here are gluten-free and will help enable you to make yourself healthy and satisfying lunches and snacks any bread eater will be jealous about. In addition, all can be easily adapted for vegan and paleo diets in addition to begin gluten-free! Be sure to substitute your favorite non-dairy versions of ingredients like:

- Yogurt
- Sour cream
- Cheese
- Milk
- Mayonnaise
- Butter

1

If you are vegan, you've probably already experimented with adapting some of your favorite recipes! An important aspect is eggs—similarly to gluten-free versions of flour, it can be difficult to recreate a dish the same without using eggs. You can substitute a flax egg using only two ingredients, and this will not only increase the health benefits of your dish, but also hold together as if you'd used chicken eggs!

1 tbsp. flaxseed meal + 2½–3 tbsp. hot water = 1 vegan egg substitute

Some of the following recipes use soy sauce, which is not always gluten-free. Be sure to double-check yours! Brands like La Choy do offer gluten-free versions, or you can simply use Tamari or coconut aminos if you prefer.

In lieu of regular bread, many recipes use real, whole foods like shredded zucchini, potato, and cucumber—these are wonderful ingredients, but you'll need to drain as much water and starch as possible before using, so it holds together properly. Once shredded, leave it to sit for a while, then use a cheesecloth or paper towels to strain and squeeze out any excess liquid.

Same with the tofu recipes—unless specifically noted, you should always drain as much water as possible so your final dish isn't waterlogged. For tofu, you can line two plates with paper towels, sandwich the tofu between them, and place a heavy object on top, like a large jar or pot. If you have time, try to switch out the paper towels a couple times to get the most liquid out.

Happy cooking!

Closed Sandwiches

Apple and Cheddar Sandwiches

Servings: 4

Ingredients

2 large apples
1 cup shredded cheddar cheese
Sprig of thyme, leaves removed
1 tbsp. melted butter
1 tsp. honey

Instructions

1. Cut apples crosswise into ½-inch thick disks. Carefully remove the seeds.
2. Mix shredded cheese with thyme leaves and spread over half of the apple slices. Cover with leftover apples.
3. Heat grill pan over medium heat. Mix butter with honey and brush apple slices with this mixture.
4. Grill on both sides until cheese has melted and grilled marks have appeared on apples.

Chicken & Ricotta Sandwich

Servings: 1

Ingredients

1 boneless, skinless chicken breast
Salt and pepper to taste
½ cup shredded mozzarella
½ cup ricotta
1 tbsp. grainy mustard
1 tsp. dried Italian herbs
¼ cup spinach leaves

Instructions

1. Season chicken breast with salt and pepper. Over medium-high heat, cook for 4 minutes on each side or until cooked through. Let sit on a plate for a couple minutes.
2. Meanwhile mix two cheeses with mustard, Italian herbs, and a pinch of salt.
3. Slice chicken breast lengthwise. Cover one of the slices with spinach leaves and cheese mixture, then place the other half of the chicken breast on top and enjoy.

Fresh Bell Pepper & Ham

Servings: 1

Ingredients

1 red bell pepper, sliced in half, deseeded
¼ cup fresh arugula
1 tbsp. grainy mustard
3 slices mozzarella cheese
4 slices smoked ham

Instructions

1. Fill one half of your pepper with arugula leaves.
2. Layer mustard, sliced mozzarella, and ham on top. Top with your second pepper slice.

Garlicky Cheese "Bread" Sandwiches

Servings: 3

Ingredients

3 eggs, separated
1½ oz. cream cheese (+ more for serving)
1 tsp. garlic powder
Pinch of salt
9 ham slices
1 cucumber, sliced

Instructions

1. Preheat oven to 300°F. Line a baking sheet with parchment paper.
2. Combine egg yolks with cream cheese, garlic powder, and a pinch of salt.
3. Whip egg whites to form stiff peaks. Carefully combine egg whites and yolk mixture with a spatula.
4. Place 6 equal portions (about 1 heaping tablespoon each) of egg mixture onto a parchment covered baking sheet. Bake for 20–25 minutes and let cool down completely.
5. Spread some cream cheese over half of the cheese "bread," top with ham, cucumbers, and another piece of "bread."

Reverse Chicken Burger

Servings: 2

Ingredients

1 lb. minced chicken
1 tsp. dried oregano
1 tsp. garlic powder
Pinch of salt
4 slices cheese (whichever is your favorite)
1 tomato, sliced
4 bacon slices, cooked
1 red onion, sliced
2 lettuce leaves

Instructions

1. Mix chicken with oregano, garlic powder, and a generous pinch of salt. Divide the mixture into 4 and form each quarter into a patty.
2. Over medium-high heat, fry chicken patties for 3–4 minutes on each side.
3. When patties are done, layer cheese, tomato, bacon, red onion, and lettuce on top of two patties and cover with the remaining two. Serve when cheese has melted.

Apple Turkey Sandwiches

Servings: 2

Ingredients

1 large apple
½ tsp. lemon juice
½ lb. turkey, minced
Pinch of salt
½ tsp. dried sage
1 garlic clove, minced
4 spinach leaves

Instructions

1. Remove apple core and slice the apple into ½-inch thick disks. Brush each with lemon juice to prevent browning.
2. Mix turkey mince with a pinch of salt, dried sage, and garlic. Form into two small patties and fry for 3 minutes on both sides.
3. Top apple slice with torn spinach leaves, place turkey patty on top, and cover with another apple slice. Repeat with leftover patty.

Smoked Tofu Banh Mi

Servings: 2

Ingredients

2 tbsp. apple cider vinegar
5 tbsp. water
1½ tsp. sugar
1 small garlic clove, minced
Pinch of red pepper flakes
½ tsp. salt
½ cup carrot, julienned
½ cup daikon, julienned
2 blocks smoked tofu, drained and pressed to remove excess moisture
2 tbsp. vegetable oil
Hot sauce for serving
1 cucumber, thinly sliced into rounds
Fresh cilantro, chopped

Instructions

1. Create your pickling liquid by combining the vinegar, water, sugar, minced garlic, red pepper flakes, and a pinch of salt.
2. Mix carrot and daikon, and cover vegetables with pickling liquid. Move to the fridge for 30 minutes.
3. Cut each brick of tofu in half lengthwise. Fry tofu in vegetable oil over medium heat until brown and crispy on both sides.
4. Drizzle one tofu slice with hot sauce. Top with sliced cucumber, pickled vegetables, fresh cilantro, and leftover tofu slice.

Turkey Salad Apple Sandwich

Servings: 2

Ingredients

1 large red apple, cored
1 cup cooked turkey meat, shredded
3 tbsp. raisins
1 tsp. fresh parsley, chopped
½ tsp. dried celery
Pinch of turmeric
3 tbsp. mayonnaise
1 tbsp. sour cream
Spinach or lettuce leaves

Instructions

1. Slice your apple into ½-inch thick rounds.
2. Make a salad by mixing shredded turkey, raisins, herbs, and spices, with mayonnaise and sour cream.
3. Place your desired amount of greens over one apple round, top with salad, and another apple slice. Repeat with another sandwich.

Caprese Sandwiches

Servings: 6

Ingredients

2 large tomatoes, sliced into ½-inch rounds
4 oz. ball fresh mozzarella, sliced into ¼-inch rounds
Salt and pepper to taste
Fresh basil leaves
Olive oil and balsamic glaze for serving

Instructions

1. Place 6 slices of mozzarella over 6 slices of tomato. Season with a pinch of salt and pepper. Add basil leaves as desired.
2. Cover with leftover tomato slices. Drizzle some balsamic vinegar and olive oil before serving. Add fresh basil leaves.

Creamy Tofu Nori Sandwich

Serving: 4

Ingredients

1 cup cooked sushi rice
1½ tbsp. rice vinegar + ½ tsp.
½ tsp. salt
½ tbsp. sugar + a pinch
2 sheets nori
1 block silky tofu
1 tsp. nutritional yeast
1 tbsp. dill, chopped
½ cup spinach leaves
1 tbsp. sesame seeds

Instructions

1. Mix sushi rice with 1½ tablespoons rice vinegar, salt, and ½ tablespoon sugar.
2. Place nori sheet shiny side down onto a piece of cling film.
3. Place half of the rice in the middle of the sheet and spread evenly with wet hands.
4. Blend tofu with a pinch of sugar, ½ teaspoon vinegar, and nutritional yeast, until creamy. Season with salt to taste. Mix in chopped dill.
5. Layer rice with spinach leaves, creamy tofu, and sprinkle sesame seeds on top.
6. Seal all corners of the nori sheet on top of the filling. Wet the nori with your fingertips if needed. Repeat with leftover ingredients.
7. Cover the sandwich with cling film, put a weight on top (such as a jar or pan) and leave for 30 minutes. Cut each sandwich in half before serving.

Mushroom Breakfast Sandwiches

Servings: 2

Ingredients

2 eggs
4 medium cremini mushrooms
1 small tomato, chopped
4 slices smoked ham
Salt and pepper to taste

Instructions

1. Poach your eggs in salted, lightly simmering water for 3 minutes. Drain onto kitchen paper.
2. Preheat your grill or stovetop to medium heat and grill mushrooms until marks appear on the surface.
3. Lay chopped tomato into each mushroom cap. Add a couple slices of ham on top and finish with poached eggs.
4. Season with salt and pepper. Top with another mushroom cap before serving.

Polenta Grilled Cheese

Servings: 2

Ingredients

1 cup instant polenta
Salt to taste
1 tbsp. olive oil
2 cups shredded mozzarella
1 tsp. dried basil

Instructions

1. Cook polenta according to package directions. Season with salt to taste.
2. Spread polenta in 8x8-inch baking pan and let set in the fridge for an hour.
3. Make polenta "bread": Cut polenta sheet into 4 squares. Over medium-high heat, fry each slice in olive oil for 1–2 minutes or until brown and crispy.
4. Flip, top 2 polenta slices with shredded mozzarella and dried basil, lower the heat, and cover with a lid. Let the cheese melt. Serve grilled cheese sandwiches immediately.

Crispy Lettuce Burger

Servings: 3

Ingredients

3 prepared beef patties
Salt and pepper to taste
1 tbsp. olive oil
3 slices of your favorite cheese
Large lettuce leaves, halved if needed
6 tomato slices
6 onion ring slices

Instructions

1. Season each patty with salt and pepper. Cook over medium heat with a little bit of olive oil for 4–5 minutes on each side. After flipping, cover each with cheese and leave it to melt.
2. Place patties over lettuce leaves (layer a few leaves if you'd like), and add tomato and onions. Add your favorite burger sauce and enjoy!

Double Down Chicken Sandwich

Servings: 2

Ingredients

1 chicken breast, sliced in half lengthwise
½ cup gluten-free flour of choice
1 tsp. paprika
½ tsp. chili powder
1¼ cups buttermilk
Pinch of salt
4 tbsp. canola oil
2 tbsp. mayonnaise
2 tbsp. ketchup
4 slices cheese
6 slices crispy bacon

Instructions

1. Pound each chicken breast half to an even thickness. Cut in half so you have 4 slices.
2. Make a batter by whisking together flour, paprika, chili powder, and buttermilk. Add a pinch of salt.
3. Dip chicken breast in batter and pat off the excess. Heat the canola oil to medium-high, and fry chicken for 2–3 minutes on each side.
4. Combine ketchup and mayo. Cover two chicken slices with sauce; add cheese and bacon. Place the other two halves on top. Keep cooking until cheese has melted.

Baked Zucchini Grilled Cheese

Servings: 2

Ingredients

2 cups zucchini, shredded
Pinch of salt
1 egg
⅔ cup gluten-free flour of choice
2 tbsp. olive oil
½ tsp. baking powder
1 cup shredded mozzarella
1 tsp. dried Italian herbs
1 tsp. garlic powder

Instructions

1. Preheat your oven to 450°F. Prepare a parchment-lined baking sheet.
2. Season zucchini with a generous pinch of salt and set aside for 5 minutes. Then, squeeze out as much excess liquid as possible from the zucchini. Stir in 1 egg, flour, olive oil, and baking powder.
3. Spread zucchini mixture over the parchment to form four equal patties, each about ¼-inch thick.
4. Bake for 15–17 minutes or until golden.
5. Mix cheese with herbs and garlic powder. Spread cheese over two of the patties. Cover with leftover two and leave the cheese to melt.

Chickpea Chicken Burgers

Servings: 4

Ingredients
For burgers:

1 cup cooked chicken, shredded
1 tsp. dried oregano
1 cup chickpea flour
½ tsp. baking powder
Pinch of salt
1 egg
½ cup non-dairy milk
Sliced red onion, tomatoes, greens for serving

For sauce:

2 tbsp. sour cream
2 tbsp. yogurt
2 tbsp. mayonnaise
1 tsp. chopped dill

Instructions

1. For the patties, combine chicken with oregano. Set aside.
2. For the buns, whisk chickpea flour with baking powder, salt, egg, and milk.
3. Spoon about 1 tablespoon at a time of the batter into preheated skillet, leaving space between each. Cook for 2 minutes, flip, and cook for 1 minute more.
4. Combine ingredients for the sauce.
5. To assemble, place your desired toppings on top of the bun, then add chicken and sauce. Cover with leftover buns.

Easy Nori Sandwich with Butterfish

Servings: 4

Ingredients

2 cups cooked sushi rice
2½ tbsp. rice vinegar
1 tsp. salt
1 tbsp. sugar
2 sheets nori
3 oz. smoked butterfish fillet, chopped finely
1 tbsp. chopped scallion
2 oz. cream cheese
1 tsp. soy sauce
¼ tsp. wasabi
Sesame seeds for serving

Instructions

1. Mix sushi rice with rice vinegar, salt, and sugar.
2. Cover each nori sheet with an even layer of cooked rice.
3. Mix chopped butterfish with scallion, cream cheese, soy sauce, and wasabi.
4. Layer fish mixture over the rice and cover with another nori sheet, rice side facing down. Wrap in plastic, put a weight on top (like a jar or pan) and leave in fridge for 30 minutes.
5. Cut into quarters and sprinkle with sesame seeds before serving.

Raw Zucchini Bites

Servings: 4

Ingredients

1 small zucchini, sliced into ¼-inch rounds
4 tsp. hummus
3–4 cherry tomatoes, sliced thinly
¼ cup fresh arugula
1 tsp. lemon juice

Instructions

1. Spread hummus over 4 zucchini rounds.
2. Top with tomato and fresh arugula. Drizzle with lemon juice and cover with another 4 zucchini rounds.

Chicken Halloumi Sandwich

Servings: 2

Ingredients

3 tbsp. olive oil
1 block halloumi cheese, sliced
Salt and pepper to taste
1 boneless, skinless chicken breast
½ lemon, juiced and zested
¼ cup pesto
6–8 spinach leaves

Instructions

1. Preheat olive oil over medium heat. Season halloumi slices with salt and pepper, then fry on both sides until golden and crispy.
2. Pound chicken breast to ½-inch thickness, cut to fit halloumi slices, then season with salt. Add lemon juice and zest. Fry for 3–4 minutes on both sides.
3. Spread pesto sauce over each chicken slice and sandwich with spinach leaves between halloumi cheese.

Vegan Ramen Burgers

Servings: 2

Ingredients

½ tbsp. olive oil
⅓ cup cremini mushrooms, chopped
1 small white onion, finely chopped
1 large garlic clove, minced
⅔ cup cooked red lentils
2 tbsp. water
⅓ cup gluten-free breadcrumbs of choice
Salt and pepper to taste
1 tsp. dried Italian herbs
2 packs instant ramen, cooked
Sliced tomatoes, lettuce, pickles, and your sauce of choice for serving

Instructions

1. Heat olive oil to medium-high. Sauté mushrooms and onion until excess liquid evaporates. Add minced garlic at the end of cooking.
2. Mash lentils using potato masher. Add water, breadcrumbs, and mushrooms. Season with salt, pepper, and dried herbs.
3. Form two round patties and fry each for 2 minutes on each side.
4. For the ramen bun, use 2½-inch metal ring. Place it on a greased pan over medium heat. Place a quarter of the cooked ramen in and fry for two minutes. Carefully remove the ring and flip the bun. Cook for 2 minutes more. Repeat with leftover ramen to make 4 buns.
5. Top half of the buns with your cooked patties and desired toppings. Cover with another bun on top.

Zucchini Panini

Servings: 4

Ingredients

1 medium zucchini, sliced lengthwise thinly
6–8 ham slices
½ cup mozzarella, shredded
½ cup gluten-free flour of choice
½ cup milk
1 cup gluten-free breadcrumbs
2 tbsp. olive oil

Instructions

1. Cover half of zucchini slices with ham and cheese. Top with more zucchini and press slightly.
2. Dredge zucchini sandwiches in flour, dip in milk, and repeat one more time. Cover with breadcrumbs.
3. Over medium-high heat, fry paninis with olive oil for 2–3 minutes on each side.

Crispy Chicken Sandwiches

Servings: 3

Ingredients

2 boneless, skinless chicken breasts, each halved lengthwise
Salt to taste
½ cup gluten-free flour of choice
1 egg, whisked
1 cup gluten-free breadcrumbs or cornflakes, crushed
1 avocado
¼ lime, juiced
1 small tomato, diced
½ small bell pepper, diced
½ small red onion, diced
½ lime, zested
1 tbsp. olive oil

Instructions

1. Pound each piece of chicken to ½-inch thickness, then season with salt. Coat with flour, then dip into beaten egg, and cover with crushed cereal or breadcrumbs. Fry for 2 minutes on each side.
2. With a fork, mash avocado with a pinch of salt and a teaspoon of lime juice.
3. Top two chicken slices with mashed avocado.
4. Mix diced vegetables with leftover lime juice and zest, add olive oil and a pinch of salt. Lay vegetable salsa on top of the avocado mash and cover with another slice of chicken.

Onigirazu Nori Sandwich

Servings: 4

Ingredients

2 cups cooked sushi rice
2½ tbsp. rice vinegar
1 tsp. salt
1 tbsp. sugar
2 sheets nori
1 tsp. lime juice
1 tbsp. soy sauce (La Choy and Tamari have gluten-free options)
½ cup pickled carrots
1 medium cucumber, seeded, thinly sliced
1 small avocado, peeled, thinly sliced

Instructions

1. Mix sushi rice with rice vinegar, salt, and sugar.
2. Cover both nori sheets with cooked rice evenly.
3. Mix soy sauce and lime juice. Lightly brush the mixture over rice.
4. Lay pickled carrots, cucumber, and sliced avocado over one of nori sheets. Place another nori sheet on top and press lightly.
5. Cut into quarters before serving.

Asian Deviled Egg Sandwich

Servings: 5

Ingredients

5 hard-boiled eggs
1 tbsp. soy sauce (La Choy and Tamari have gluten-free options)
1 tsp. wasabi
1 tbsp. Kewpie Japanese mayonnaise
1 oz. konnyaku noodles
1 tbsp. sweet and sour sauce
Salt to taste
Green onion, chili flakes, sriracha, sesame seeds for serving

Instructions

1. Cut each boiled egg in half and remove the yolk.
2. Blend all the yolks with soy sauce, wasabi, and mayonnaise. Add salt to taste.
3. Mix sweet and sour sauce with the noodles.
4. Fill half of the egg whites with noodles and another half with egg yolk mixture. Add your toppings of choice, and sandwich right before eating.

"Meringue Bun" Sandwiches

Servings: 2

Ingredients

4 egg whites
¼ tsp. white wine vinegar
Generous pinch of salt
2 slices of your favorite cheese
4 slices of ham
¼ cup fresh arugula

Instructions

1. Preheat your oven to 450°F. Prepare a parchment-covered baking sheet.
2. Beat your egg whites with vinegar and a generous pinch of salt until stiff peaks form.
3. Place four portions of the beaten eggs over a parchment-covered baking sheet.
4. Bake for 3–4 minutes or until slightly golden.
5. Sandwich cheese, sliced ham, and greens between two egg "buns."

Open Sandwiches

Bell Pepper Tuna Sandwich

Servings: 2

Ingredients

1 can tuna, drained
2 tbsp. red onion, minced
1 tsp. chopped capers
1 tbsp. cream cheese
1 tbsp. sour cream
1 tbsp. mayonnaise
Salt and pepper to taste
1 red bell pepper, sliced in half and deseeded
Fresh parsley for garnish

Instructions

1. Combine tuna, red onion, and chopped capers. Add cream cheese, sour cream, and mayo. Season with salt and pepper to taste.
2. Stuff bell pepper halves with tuna salad and garnish with fresh chopped parsley.

Halloumi Breakfast Sandwich

Servings: 2

Ingredients

1 block halloumi cheese, sliced in half
3 eggs
1 tsp. cornstarch
2 tbsp. cream
2 tbsp. olive oil
1 bell pepper, thinly sliced
1 cup spinach

Instructions

1. Fry halloumi slices over medium heat until golden on both sides.
2. Whisk 3 eggs with cream and cornstarch.
3. In a pan, heat olive oil and sauté sliced pepper until softened. Add spinach and cook until wilted.
4. Pour eggs over veggies and start stir slowly with a spatula until eggs look nice and creamy but slightly underdone.
5. Place scrambled eggs onto halloumi, drizzle some olive oil, and season with freshly ground pepper.

Smoked Salmon Cheese "Bread" Sandwiches

Servings: 6

Ingredients

6 cheese "breads" (recipe on page 10)
2 tbsp. butter, room temperature
1 tsp. fresh dill, chopped
1 tsp. lemon zest
Salt to taste
6–9 slices smoked salmon

Instructions

1. Mix butter with fresh dill and lemon zest. Season with salt.
2. Smear aromatic butter on top of each "bread" slice and layer salmon over. Garnish with more fresh dill and a lemon wedge if desired.

Spicy Tofu Sandwich

Servings: 2

Ingredients

1 package extra-firm tofu
1 tsp. fresh ginger, minced
1 tsp. fresh garlic, minced
4 tbsp. light soy sauce (make sure it's gluten-free)
½ tsp. red pepper flakes
2 tbsp. vegetable oil
5–6 spinach leaves
½ avocado, sliced
$2/3$ cup cooked chicken breast, shredded
2 tbsp. mayonnaise
2 tsp. sriracha

Instructions

1. Press tofu with paper towels to remove any excess moisture. Cut in half lengthwise.
2. Mix minced garlic, ginger, soy sauce, and pepper flakes. Brush tofu slices with marinade. Leave for 15 minutes at room temperature.
3. Fry marinated tofu with vegetable oil over medium-high heat for 2 minutes on each side or until brown and crispy.
4. Top each tofu slice with spinach leaves, avocado, and shredded chicken. Combine sriracha and mayo, and drizzle on top.

Caramelized Onion Mushroom Sandwiches

Servings 2

Ingredients

4 large cremini mushroom caps
2 tbsp. butter
2 medium white onions, sliced into $\frac{1}{8}$-inch rings
½ tsp. dried thyme
Pinch of salt
1 tbsp. sugar
¼ cup vegetable broth
1 cup vegan "ground beef"

Instructions

1. Preheat your grill over medium heat. Grill mushroom caps, pressing down slightly. When mushrooms are brown and crispy, remove from heat.
2. In a pan, melt your butter and sauté onions over low heat. When onions are translucent, add thyme, a pinch of salt, sugar, and 2 tablespoons vegetable broth.
3. Leave onions to caramelize for 10–15 minutes, adding more broth as needed.
4. Add in "ground beef," check for seasoning, and adjust to taste.
5. Layer onion mixture over two mushroom caps and cover with leftover mushrooms.

Beet and Lentil Sandwiches

Servings: 4

Ingredients

1 cup red lentils, cooked and mashed
1 small beet, cooked and pureed
2 tbsp. gluten-free flour of choice
¼ cup gluten-free breadcrumbs
1 garlic clove, minced
Salt to taste
1 tsp. vegetable oil
½ cup arugula
1 tbsp. olive oil
1 tbsp. lemon juice
¼ cup goat cheese
2 tbsp. pumpkin seeds

Instructions

1. Mix lentil and beet puree together. Add flour, breadcrumbs, minced garlic, and salt to the mixture.
2. Form lentil mixture into 4 patties.
3. Heat vegetable oil over medium heat and cook patties for 2 minutes on each side.
4. Season arugula with salt, olive oil, and lemon juice. Place simple salad over each patty; top with crumbled goat cheese and pumpkin seeds.

Potato Latke Breakfast Sandwiches

Servings: 4

Ingredients

2 medium potatoes (about 1 cup), shredded and squeezed of excess moisture
¼ cup gluten-free flour of choice
5 eggs
4 slices cooked bacon
A pinch of salt and pepper

Instructions

1. Preheat your oven to 400°F.
2. Mix shredded potatoes with flour and one of the eggs. Using a muffin tin, fill 4 wells with potato mixture, spreading it with your fingers over the bottom and sides.
3. Bake the cups for 8–10 minutes until golden.
4. Layer each potato cup with bacon and crack one egg on top of each. Season and bake for 8 minutes more.

Rice Cake Pizza

Servings: 4

Ingredients

2 cups cooked rice
1 egg
2 tbsp. shredded Parmesan
1 tsp. dried basil
¼ cup gluten-free flour of choice
Salt to taste
1 tbsp. olive oil
12 salami slices
2 tbsp. store-bought tomato sauce
½ cup shredded mozzarella or other pizza cheese
Fresh basil for serving

Instructions

1. Combine cooked rice with the egg, shredded Parmesan, basil, flour, and a pinch of salt.
2. Heat olive oil over medium heat. Divide mixture into 4 patties about ½-inch thick. Fry in the oil until golden on both sides.
3. When almost done, spread tomato sauce over one side of each rice cake; add cheese and salami.
4. Serve warm, topped with fresh basil.

Grilled Bell Pepper & Mozzarella

Servings: 2

Ingredients

1 tbsp. olive oil
1 cup button mushrooms, sliced
½ small white onion, sliced
1 grilled red pepper, sliced in half and deseeded
½ cup tomatoes, chopped
½ cup mozzarella, shredded
Fresh basil and balsamic glaze for garnish

Instructions

1. Preheat olive oil over medium heat and sauté sliced mushrooms and onion for 5–7 minutes.
2. Lay mushrooms and onion over grilled peppers; top with tomatoes and mozzarella cheese.
3. Broil until cheese has melted and garnish with fresh basil and balsamic glaze before serving.

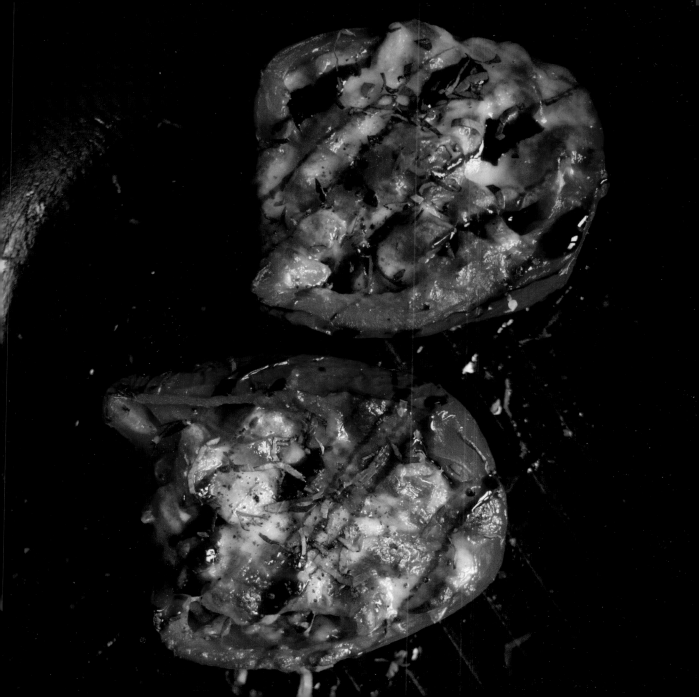

Crispy Onion Cups

Servings: 10–12

Ingredients

2–3 small white onions, sliced in quarters
¼ cup gluten-free flour of choice
½ cup non-dairy milk
½ cup gluten-free breadcrumbs
1 cup vegan "ground beef"
3–4 cremini mushrooms, chopped
Salt to taste
2 garlic cloves, minced
2 tbsp. fresh parsley, chopped
¼ cup store-bought tomato sauce

Instructions

1. Preheat your oven to 400°F. Prepare a parchment-covered baking sheet.
2. Carefully separate each layer of each onion quarter. Sprinkle each onion "petal" with flour, dip in milk, and cover with breadcrumbs.
3. Layer onion cups over the prepared sheet and bake for 20 minutes.
4. Meanwhile, sauté vegan beef with mushrooms until cooked through. Season with salt and stir in minced garlic, tomato sauce, and parsley.
5. Fill each onion cup with mince and serve sprinkled with parsley.

Lentil Pancake Sandwiches

Servings: 5

Ingredients

1 cup red/orange lentils, cooked and mashed
1 egg
2 tbsp. gluten-free flour of choice
2 tbsp. milk of choice
1 tsp. baking powder
Pinch of salt
1 cup broccoli florets
½ cup red onion, chopped
½ cup bell pepper, chopped
1 garlic clove, minced
¼ cup water
½ tsp. curry powder
Yogurt for serving

Instructions

1. Combine pureed lentils with egg, flour, and milk. Add baking powder and generous pinch of salt. Divide into patties.
2. Cook patties over medium heat for 2 minutes on each side.
3. In another pan, sauté chopped vegetables over medium heat for 4–5 minutes. Season with curry powder and salt. Add minced garlic and ¼ cup of water. Let the vegetables steam until all the liquid evaporates.
4. Place curried vegetables over lentil pancake and drizzle with yogurt before serving.

Lentil and Herbed Mushrooms Pancake

Servings: 7

Ingredients

1 cup red lentils, cooked
Salt and pepper to taste
1 small egg
¼ cup white onion, chopped
2 tbsp. parsley, chopped
1 tbsp. butter
2 cups assorted mushrooms, chopped
2 garlic cloves, minced
1 tsp. Herbes de Provence
2 tbsp. white wine
Balsamic glaze for serving

Ingredients

1. Mash cooked lentil with potato masher. Season and combine with egg, onion, and parsley.
2. Divide into 7 even patties and fry for 2–3 minutes on each side.
3. In a separate pan over medium, melt butter and sauté mushrooms in it. Season with salt, garlic, and herbs, pour some wine in, and let it boil away.
4. Top each lentil patty with mushrooms and serve drizzled with balsamic glaze.

Olive Tapenade Baked Zucchini Bites

Servings: 6

Ingredients

1 medium zucchini, shredded
2 tbsp. flax meal
½ cup gluten-free flour of choice
1 tsp. dried basil
Salt to taste
⅓ cup green olives
1 tbsp. capers
1 garlic clove
1 tbsp. olive oil
¼ tsp. lemon zest
½ tsp. lemon juice
2 tbsp. red bell pepper, chopped

Instructions

1. Preheat oven to 400°F.
2. Squeeze out as much moisture from the zucchini as possible. Mix shredded zucchini with flax meal, flour, basil, and salt.
3. Scoop the dough and form 6 small patties. Place each on a parchment-covered baking sheet. Bake for 20 minutes.
4. For the tapenade, chop olives, capers, and garlic, and combine with olive oil. Add lemon juice and zest along with the bell pepper. Spread tapenade over the cooled zucchini patties.

Onion "Bun" Sandwich with Creamy Dill Pickle Salad

Servings: 4

Ingredients

½ cup gluten-free flour of choice (+ more for dredging)
¼ tsp. baking powder
Pinch of salt
½ cup cold soda water
1 large white onion, sliced into ¼-inch rounds
Canola oil for frying
½ cup cornichons, chopped
¼ cup red radishes, chopped
1 tbsp. chopped dill
2 tbsp. non-dairy sour cream

Instructions

1. Mix flour, baking powder, salt, and cold soda until no lumps remain.
2. Dip each onion ring into the batter and fry in preheated canola oil for
   2–3 minutes or until crispy.
3. Combine cornichons, radishes, dill, and non-dairy sour cream. Season with salt
   to taste.
4. Top each onion ring with pickle salad and serve immediately.

Sweet Potato Patties with Tomato Chutney

Servings: 4

Ingredients

For the patties:
1 medium sweet potato, washed and dried
1 tsp. olive oil
$^2/_3$ cup gluten-free breadcrumbs
Salt and ground black pepper to taste
1 tsp. smoked paprika
½ tsp. ground coriander
1 tbsp. cilantro, chopped
2 garlic cloves, minced
1 tsp. vegetable oil

For the chutney:
2 medium tomatoes, chopped
½ tsp. turmeric
1 tsp. ginger-garlic paste
Pinch of chili powder
Pinch of salt

Instructions

1. Preheat your oven to 400°F. Poke the sweet potato all over with a fork and brush with olive oil. Bake for 45–50 minutes or until tender. Let cool down.
2. Peel and mash baked potato. Season with salt, pepper, paprika, coriander, cilantro, and garlic.
3. Divide into 4 patties and fry with some vegetable oil until golden on both sides.
4. In another pan, fry tomatoes until mushy. Pulse with a blender and season with turmeric, ginger-garlic paste, chili powder, and salt. Top the patties with the mixture.

Mushroom Pizza Sandwich

Servings: 3

Ingredients

6 medium cremini mushrooms, cleaned, stems removed
3 tbsp. tomato sauce
½ cup red peppers, chopped
¼ cup black olives, sliced
½ cup mixed vegan cheese
Fresh basil for serving

Instructions

1. Preheat oven to 400°F.
2. Fill each mushroom cap with pizza sauce.
3. Layer red pepper, olives, and cheese on top. You may use other toppings of your choice.
4. Bake for 8–10 minutes and serve sprinkled with fresh basil.

Halloumi Bruschetta

Servings: 9

Ingredients

1 block halloumi cheese, sliced in thirds lengthwise
2 tbsp. olive oil
2 tbsp. fresh basil, chopped
1 large tomato, chopped
1 small red onion, chopped
1 small bell pepper, chopped
1 tbsp. lemon juice
Salt and pepper to taste
Balsamic glaze for serving

Instructions

1. Slice halloumi cheese and pan fry it on a lightly oiled pan until golden on both sides. Cut each slice diagonally.
2. Meanwhile combine mixed vegetables, olive oil, and lemon juice. Season with salt and pepper to taste.
3. Top each halloumi slice with vegetable mixture and drizzle balsamic glaze on top.

Cauliflower Breakfast Cups

Servings: 6

Ingredients

1½ cups steamed cauliflower, shredded
7 eggs
1 tbsp. olive oil
½ cup gluten-free breadcrumbs
Salt and pepper to taste

Instructions

1. Preheat your oven to 400°F. Grease muffin tin cups with some vegetable oil or cooking spray.
2. Combine cauliflower, 1 egg, olive oil, and breadcrumbs. Season with salt and pepper.
3. Spoon cauliflower mixture into each muffin tin cup and press onto bottoms and sides of the cups.
4. Bake for 15 minutes. Then, crack one egg into each cup and continue cooking for 10–15 minutes until eggs are cooked through.

Spicy Chickpea Chicken Sandwiches

Servings: 4

Ingredients

2 cups chickpeas, cooked
1 small egg
4 tbsp. gluten-free flour of choice
2 tbsp. gluten-free breadcrumbs of choice
2 tbsp. olive oil
2 garlic cloves, minced
2 tbsp. white onion, chopped
1 cup chicken, minced or chopped
½ tsp. chopped jalapeño pepper
¼ cup chicken broth
1 tbsp. tomato paste
2 tbsp. canned corn
Handful of mixed greens
1 tsp. lemon juice
Salt and pepper to taste

Instructions

1. Blend or mash chickpeas to form a paste. Season with salt, add a small egg, and the flour, and combine. Add the breadcrumbs here, if using.
2. Heat olive oil and fry each patty for 2 minutes on each side.
3. In another pan, sauté the garlic and onion until translucent. Add minced chicken and chopped pepper. Season with salt and cook for 3 minutes.
4. Mix chicken broth with tomato paste and pour the sauce over minced chicken. Stir in the corn. Cook for 2 minutes more.
5. Drizzle mixed greens with some lemon juice.
6. Top each patty with greens and minced meat. Serve warm.

Rice Cakes with Tomatoes and Cottage Cheese

Servings: 4

Ingredients

2 cups cooked rice
½ cup cheese, shredded
1 egg
4 tbsp. gluten-free flour of choice
3 tbsp. olive oil
8 cherry tomatoes, cut in quarters
1 tsp. lemon juice
½ cup cottage cheese
1 tbsp. chopped parsley
Salt and pepper to taste

Instructions

1. Combine cooked rice with shredded cheese, egg, and flour.
2. Heat 1 tablespoon olive oil. Divide rice mixture into 4 rice cakes and fry each one for 2 minutes on both sides or until golden.
3. Season tomatoes with lemon juice, remaining olive oil, salt, and pepper.
4. Season cottage cheese with salt and stir chopped parsley in.
5. Spread cottage cheese over rice cakes. Top with tomatoes and serve immediately.

Sweet Potato Latkes with Creamy Tzatziki

Servings: 4

Ingredients

For the latkes:
½ medium sweet potato, shredded
1 small egg
½ small white onion, minced
½ cup gluten-free flour of choice
Salt and pepper to taste
2 tbsp. olive oil

For the tzatziki:
½ cup strained yogurt
1 tsp. dill, chopped
1 small cucumber, shredded and squeezed of excess moisture
1 small garlic clove, minced
Olive oil to taste

Instructions

1. Mix potato, egg, onion, and flour together. Season with salt and pepper to taste.
2. Heat a skillet with olive oil over medium heat. Make eight small latkes and fry each until crispy and golden on both sides. Absorb excess grease with paper towels.
3. Mix all tzatziki ingredients together and top latkes with it.

Falafel Sandwiches

Servings: 4

Ingredients

2 cups canned chickpeas
¼ cup walnuts
2 tbsp. white onion, chopped
2 garlic cloves, minced
1 tsp. ground cumin
1 tsp. paprika
1 tbsp. parsley, chopped
¼ cup vegetable oil
1 cucumber, chopped small
1 tomato, chopped
1 tsp. dill, chopped
¼ cup non-dairy yogurt
¼ white onion, thinly sliced
Salt to taste

Instructions

1. Using a blender, beat together chickpeas, walnuts, chopped onion, garlic, cumin, and paprika. Add salt to taste. Mix with parsley.
2. Divide mixture into 4 and form patties.
3. Fry each patty in preheated vegetable oil for 2 minutes on each side. Lay over paper towels.
4. Combine cucumbers, tomatoes, and dill with yogurt. Season with salt.
5. Top each falafel patty with this salad and thinly sliced onion rings.

Baked Avocado Breakfast "Boats"

Servings: 2

Ingredients

1 large avocado
2 tbsp. sour cream
2 tbsp. cheese, shredded or torn
2 egg yolks
Salt and pepper to taste

Instructions

1. Preheat your oven to 350°F.
2. Cut avocado in half and remove the pit. Scoop about $^2/_3$ of the "meat" out.
3. Mash scooped avocado with fork. Season with salt and pepper, then add sour cream and cheese to it.
4. Fill each avocado half with cheesy filling, leaving a well for the egg yolk in the middle.
5. Top each avocado with a yolk and bake for 8–10 minutes.

Avocado Chicken Melts

Servings: 4

Ingredients

2 medium avocados
1 cup cooked chicken breast, shredded
1 tbsp. capers, chopped
2 tbsp. mayonnaise
1 tbsp. green onion, chopped
A pinch of salt

Instructions

1. Preheat your oven to 350°F.
2. Cut avocados in half and remove the pits. Scoop about $^2/_3$ of the "meat" out of each.
3. Mash the scooped avocado and mix it with shredded chicken, chopped capers, and mayonnaise. Season with salt to taste.
4. Fill each avocado shell with chicken mixture and bake for 12–15 minutes.
5. Sprinkle with onion before serving.

Rolls and Wraps

Crab Cucumber Roll-Ups

Servings: 4

Ingredients

1 large cucumber
½ cup shredded crab meat
2 tbsp. cream cheese
1 tbsp. mayonnaise
1 garlic clove, minced
1 tbsp. dill, chopped

Instructions

1. Using a vegetable peeler or mandoline, slice cucumber into thin strips lengthwise.
2. Mix crab meat with cream cheese, mayonnaise, minced garlic, and dill.
3. Spread about 1 tablespoon of crab filling over each cucumber strip and roll it up tightly.

Crispy Oyster Mushroom Lettuce Wraps

Servings: 3

Ingredients

½ cup gluten-free flour of choice (+ more for dredging)
¼ tsp. baking power
Pinch of salt
½ cup cold soda
1 cup oyster mushrooms, sliced into ¼-inch strips
1 cup vegetable oil
3 lettuce leaves
½ cup sweet and sour sauce
¼ cup roasted peanuts, chopped
Lime, fresh green onion, chili flakes for serving

Instructions

1. Mix flour, baking powder, salt, and cold soda to make a smooth batter.
2. Dredge oyster mushrooms in plain flour first, shaking off any excess. Dip mushrooms in batter and fry in batches in preheated vegetable oil for 2–3 minutes or until crispy.
3. Fill each lettuce leaf with mushrooms, and drizzle with sauce and chopped nuts. Add green onion, chili flakes, and lime juice before serving.

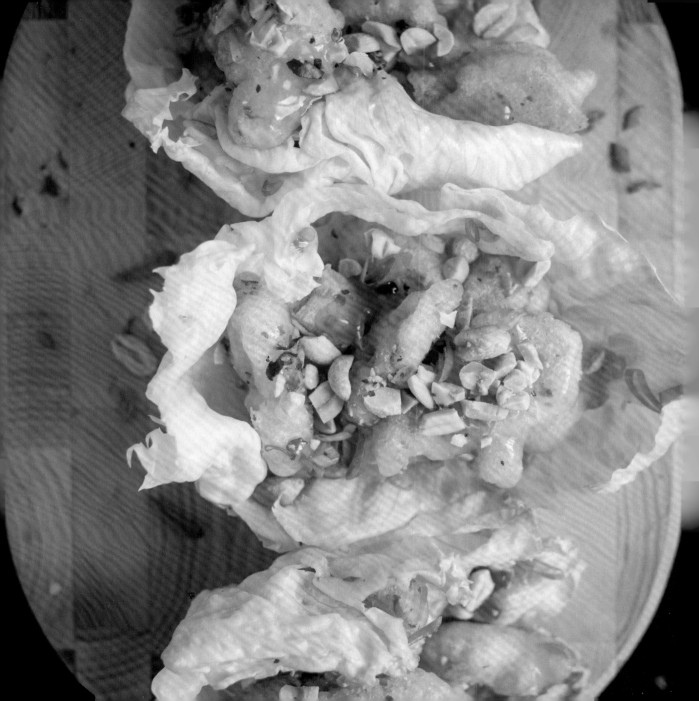

Brown Rice Burritos

Servings: 2

Ingredients

2/3 cup cooked brown rice
½ cup canned red beans
½ cup canned corn
2 tbsp. cilantro, chopped
½ lime, juiced
1 medium tomato, chopped
2 tbsp. red onion, finely chopped
Pinch of salt
2 gluten-free tortillas

Instructions

1. Mix cooked brown rice with beans, corn, cilantro, lime juice, tomato, and onion. Season with salt to taste.
2. Top each tortilla with burrito filling and wrap as tightly as possible.

Hummus Wraps

Servings: 2

Ingredients

2 gluten-free tortillas
½ cup hummus
6–8 spinach leaves
1 medium tomato, thinly sliced
1 red bell pepper, sliced into thin strips
²/₃ cup purple cabbage, shredded
¹/₃ cup sour cream

Instructions

1. Spread ¼ cup of hummus over each tortilla. Layer greens, tomato, and bell pepper on top. Mix shredded cabbage with sour cream and top each tortilla.
2. Roll as tightly as possible and wrap in paper.

Sweet and Sour Tofu Lettuce Wraps

Servings: 3

Ingredients

1 tbsp. vegetable oil
3 lettuce leaves
1 block firm tofu, cut into ¼-inch cubes
1 tbsp. ginger-garlic paste
1 small shallot, minced
½ tsp. cornstarch
¼ cup water
½ tbsp. brown sugar
2 tbsp. soy sauce (make sure it's a gluten-free version!)
2 tsp. rice vinegar
¼ cup roasted peanuts, chopped
Scallions, for serving

Instructions

1. Heat vegetable oil in a pan over medium heat. Fry tofu cubes until crispy for about 4 minutes.
2. In another skillet fry ginger-garlic paste with minced shallots for 30 seconds. Mix cornstarch into cold water. To the skillet, add brown sugar, soy sauce, vinegar, and your cornstarch slurry.
3. When the sauce starts to bubble, stir in crispy tofu and peanuts.
4. Fill lettuce leaves with tofu and sauce; top with scallions before serving.

Grilled Veggie Wraps

Servings: 2

Ingredients

2 tbsp. olive oil
1 large bell pepper
½ red onion, cut into ½-inch slices
1 small zucchini, sliced lengthwise thinly
2 gluten-free tortillas
Fresh arugula, balsamic glaze for serving

Instructions

1. Preheat a cast-iron grill pan and brush it with a tablespoon of olive oil.
2. Grill bell pepper until softened and charred on the outside. Remove any seeds and skin and cut into ½-inch strips.
3. Grill onions and zucchini separately until softened.
4. Layer grilled vegetables over tortillas, top with fresh arugula, then drizzle leftover olive oil and balsamic glaze on top.

Smoked Salmon Roll-up Bites

Servings: 4

Ingredients

4 slices smoked salmon, sliced in half
¼ cup cream cheese
1/3 tsp. garlic powder
1 tsp. lemon juice
1 tbsp. olive oil
¼ cup fresh arugula

Instructions

1. For the filling, combine cream cheese with garlic, lemon juice, and olive oil.
2. Finely chop arugula until it resembles a pesto.
3. Add arugula to the cream cheese and combine.
4. Spread cream cheese over each salmon slice and roll tightly. Secure with a toothpick if needed.

Creamy Tuna Lettuce Wraps

Servings: 3

Ingredients

1 (6 oz.) can tuna
½ medium avocado, mashed
¼ cup cream cheese
1 tsp. lemon juice
1 tsp. lemon zest
1 tsp. Dijon mustard
Salt to taste
3 lettuce leaves
Canned corn, chopped tomato, or cucumber for serving

Instructions

1. Mix tuna with mashed avocado, cream cheese, lemon juice and zest, and Dijon mustard. Season with salt to taste.
2. Fill each lettuce leaf with tuna salad and top with mixed vegetables of choice, like chopped tomatoes, cucumber, and corn.

Rice Paper Omelet Sandwich Rolls

Servings: 4

Ingredients

4 eggs
4 rice paper sheets, soaked
1 bell pepper, sliced thinly
1 cucumber, sliced thinly
1 carrot, sliced thinly
2 lettuce leaves
2 tbsp. sweet and sour sauce
Salt and pepper to taste

Instructions

1. Whisk eggs with a pinch of salt and pepper.
2. In a preheated pan, pour half of the eggs and tilt the pan to make a thin omelet. When the omelet sets, transfer onto a rice paper sheet and top with the vegetables and sauce.
3. Fold both sides of the rice paper sheet and roll tightly. Repeat with leftover ingredients.

Korean Eggplant Rolls

Servings: 5

Ingredients

1 medium eggplant, sliced lengthwise thinly
½ small bell pepper, sliced thinly
¼ cup Napa cabbage, sliced thinly
¼ cup carrot, shredded
½ cup cucumber, sliced thinly
3 tbsp. peanut butter
3 tsp. soy sauce (check that it is gluten-free!)
¼ cup water
1 tbsp. rice vinegar
Pinch of brown sugar
Salt to taste

Instructions

1. Heat eggplant slices over medium heat for 1–2 minutes, seasoning with a pinch of salt.
2. Layer some vegetables on one side of the eggplant strip and roll tightly. Secure with a toothpick if needed.
3. For the dipping sauce, whisk together peanut butter, soy sauce, water, rice vinegar, and a bit of brown sugar.
4. Serve eggplant rolls with the dipping sauce.

Japanese Loaded Omelet Breakfast Roll

Servings: 1

Ingredients

½ chicken breast, cubed
1 small onion, chopped
1 cup mixed frozen vegetables
1 garlic clove, minced
2 tbsp. soy sauce (check that it is gluten-free)
¼ cup water
2 large eggs
2 tbsp. milk of choice
Ketchup for serving

Instructions

1. Cook your cubed chicken breast over the medium heat until there is no pink left. Add chopped onion and cook for 2 minutes more.
2. Mix frozen vegetables and garlic in. Season with soy sauce. Cook for 3 minutes or until vegetables are cooked through. Add ¼ cup of water, cover with a lid, and leave vegetables to steam until they are soft.
3. Beat eggs with milk and a pinch of salt. Pour into a pan over low heat to make a thin omelet. Cook until the bottom is set.
4. Top the omelet with chicken and vegetables and fold both sides of it to cover the toppings. Flip on a plate and serve with some ketchup.

Eggplant Rolls with Garlic-Walnut Filling

Servings: 5

Ingredients

1 medium eggplant
Sea salt
1 tsp. vegetable oil
1 cup walnuts, ground
1 tbsp. mayonnaise
3–4 tbsp. water
2 garlic cloves, minced
2 tbsp. cilantro, chopped

Instructions

1. Cut eggplant lengthwise into 5 even slices. Sprinkle with salt and leave for 20 minutes. Wash under cold water and dry with paper towels.
2. Fry over medium heat with some vegetable oil for 2–3 minutes or until soft and golden.
3. Combine ground walnuts with mayo, water, garlic, and cilantro to make a paste. Season with salt if needed.
4. Put about a tablespoon of filling onto an eggplant slice and roll tightly. Repeat to use all the eggplant slices and filling.

Smoked Ham Guacamole Roll-ups

Servings: 4

Ingredients

1 large avocado, cut in half and pit removed
1 tsp. lemon juice
1 tbsp. white onion, diced
2 tbsp. red bell pepper, diced
Salt and pepper to taste
Green onion for serving
4 large slices of smoked ham

Instructions

1. Scoop out the flesh of your avocado. Mash avocado with lemon juice, and a pinch of salt and pepper. Add onion and bell pepper.
2. Place a couple tablespoons of guacamole over each slice of ham, roll, and tie with green onion.

Smoked Ham and Cornichon Rolls

Servings: 5

Ingredients

¼ cup cream cheese
1 tsp. lemon juice
½ tsp. lemon zest
1 tsp. grainy mustard
1 tsp. chopped parsley
5 sliced of smoked ham
5 cornichons

Instructions

1. Combine cream cheese with lemon juice and zest. Add mustard and chopped parsley.
2. Spread cream cheese filling over each smoked ham slice. Top each with a cornichon, roll up tightly, and cut in half.

One-Bite Sandwiches

One-Bite Tofu Sandwiches

Servings: 3

Ingredients

2 tbsp. peanut oil
1 block extra firm tofu
¼ cup milk
¼ cup cornstarch
½ small avocado, diced
½ lb. cooked shrimp, diced
¼ cup mayonnaise
½ tsp. garlic powder
1 tsp. light soy sauce (check that it's gluten-free!)
Sliced green onions for serving

Instructions

1. Heat a pan with peanut oil over medium heat.
2. Cut tofu lengthwise, then cut crosswise to get about 1½ x 1½-inch squares. Soak each square in milk and coat with cornstarch mixed with a pinch of fine salt.
3. Fry for 2–3 minutes or until crispy and golden on both sides.
4. Mix diced avocado, shrimp, mayo, garlic powder, and soy sauce.
5. Top each tofu slice with shrimp salad and garnish with sliced green onions.

One-Bite Polenta Sandwiches with Creamy Mushrooms

Servings: 3

Ingredients

1 polenta "bread" sheet (page 26)
1 tbsp. olive oil
1 small white onion, chopped
2 cups oyster mushrooms, chopped
1 tbsp. butter
Pinch of salt
¼ tsp. ground nutmeg
1½ cups almond milk
1 tbsp. tapioca flour
Fresh arugula for serving

Instructions

1. Cut polenta sheet into six 2-inch rounds with a cookie cutter.
2. Preheat a pan with olive oil over medium heat. Fry each round in preheated olive oil until brown and crispy.
3. Sauté onion and mushrooms with butter until any excess mushroom liquid evaporates. Season with salt and nutmeg.
4. Stir tapioca flour into almond milk and pour the mixture over the mushrooms. Let simmer for 3–4 minutes or until thickened.
5. Spoon creamy mushrooms over each polenta round, then top with arugula.

Quick Cracker & Cheese Sandwiches

Servings: 6–8

Ingredients

4 oz. feta cheese
3 oz. sour cream
1 tbsp. dill, chopped
¼ tsp. oregano
2–3 garlic cloves, minced
Seed crackers (page 156)

Instructions

1. Whip feta cheese and sour cream together. Add dill, oregano, and minced garlic.
2. Chill for 30 minutes then serve over crackers.

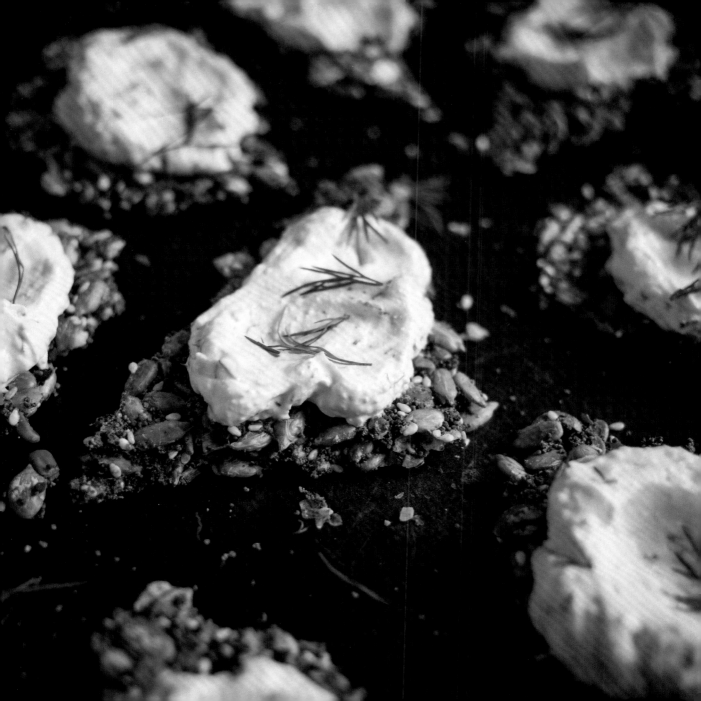

Tomato Pasta Salad Sandwiches

Servings: 6

Ingredients

6 cherry tomatoes
1 cup cooked gluten-free elbow pasta
1 tbsp. pesto
1 tsp. lemon juice
1 tsp. olive oil
1 tbsp. red onion, finely chopped

Instructions

1. Cut tomatoes in half lengthwise and remove seeds with a teaspoon.
2. Mix your pasta with pesto sauce, lemon juice, olive oil, and chopped red onion.
3. Fill tomatoes with pasta salad and secure both halves together using toothpicks.

Hummus and Olives Crispy Chicory Bites

Servings: 4

Ingredients

4 chicory leaves
4 tbsp. plain hummus
¼ cup olives, chopped
2 tbsp. walnuts, chopped
Olive oil, chopped parsley, pepper flakes for serving

Instructions

1. Spoon the hummus into each chicory boat. Top with chopped olives and nuts.
2. Drizzle with olive oil and add parsley and pepper flakes before serving.

One-Bite Cherry Tomato Sandwiches

Servings: 6

Ingredients

6 quail eggs, boiled, chopped
1 tbsp. capers, chopped
½ tsp. canned jalapeño peppers, chopped
¼ tsp. paprika
¼ cup mayonnaise
Salt to taste
6 cherry tomatoes, sliced in half crosswise
6 spinach leaves

Instructions

1. Mix your chopped quail eggs with capers, peppers, paprika, and mayonnaise. Season with salt to taste.
2. Cover half of tomato slices with spinach leaves, then top with egg salad and leftover tomatoes. Secure with toothpicks.

Eggplant Stacks with Feta Cream

Servings: 3

Ingredients

1 medium eggplant, sliced into ½-inch thick rounds
Generous pinch of salt
2 tbsp. vegetable oil
3 oz. feta cheese
1 tbsp. sour cream
1 tbsp. purple basil, chopped
1 garlic clove, minced

Instructions

1. Sprinkle eggplant rounds with salt and leave for 20 minutes. Rinse under cold water and pat dry with paper towels.
2. Fry eggplant rounds with some vegetable oil over medium heat for 2 minutes per side.
3. Combine feta with sour cream, basil, and minced garlic.
4. Top one eggplant slice with some feta cream; cover with another eggplant and some more cream. Finish with another fried eggplant round.
5. Repeat with leftover eggplants and cream to make two more stacks.

Quick Cucumber Sandwiches

Servings: 5–6

Ingredients

1 large cucumber
¼ cup dill cream cheese
6 slices smoked ham

Instructions

1. Cut cucumber in half lengthwise and remove any seeds with a teaspoon.
2. Fill one cucumber "boat" with cream cheese and another with sliced ham. Sandwich both cucumber halves and cut into bite-size pieces.

Cauliflower Bites with Cheese Spread

Servings: 6

Ingredients

1½ cups cauliflower, shredded
1 small egg
²/₃ cup gluten-free flour of choice
1 tsp. mixed Italian herbs
Pinch of salt
²/₃ cup sharp cheese, shredded
2 tbsp. mayonnaise
2 tbsp. cream cheese
1 tsp. garlic powder
½ tsp. mustard

Instructions

1. Heat your oven to 350°F. Grease a muffin tin with vegetable oil.
2. Combine cauliflower with egg, flour, and herbs. Add a pinch of salt.
3. Fill six muffin cups with the cauliflower mixture and bake for 20–25 minutes. Leave to cool afterwards.
4. Meanwhile, make your cheese spread. Mix shredded cheese with mayo, cream cheese, garlic powder, and mustard. Season with salt if needed.
5. Spread the cheese over each cauliflower patty before serving.

Blue Cheese Chicory Boats

Servings: 4

Ingredients

3 oz. blue cheese, crumbled
2 tbsp. dried cranberries
½ pear, cut into small cubes
4 chicory leaves
Honey for serving

Instructions

1. Mix crumbled cheese with dried cranberries and pear.
2. Fill each chicory leaf with the mixture. Drizzle with honey before serving.

Pickled Cucumber Bites with Mackerel Salad

Servings: 10

Ingredients

½ can mackerel
2 tbsp. mayonnaise
1 tbsp. white onion, finely chopped
1 hard-boiled egg, finely chopped
1 large pickled cucumber, sliced into ¼-inch thick rounds

Instructions

1. For the mackerel salad, use a fork to mash mackerel with mayonnaise.
2. Add white onion and hard-boiled egg. Stir to combine.
3. Sandwich fish salad between two pickle slices. Repeat to use up all the fish.

Skewers

Caprese Skewers

Servings: 5

Ingredients

10 small mozzarella balls
10 cherry tomatoes, halved
½ cup basil leaves
Olive oil, balsamic glaze for serving

Instructions

1. Skewer mozzarella, cherry tomatoes, and basil leaves.
2. Drizzle with olive oil and balsamic glaze before serving.

Quick Antipasto Skewers

Servings: 4

Ingredients

1 tbsp. olive oil
½ cup pickled cremini mushrooms
$1/8$ cup green olives
1 cup cherry tomatoes, halved
8 spinach leaves

Instructions

1. Skewer all ingredients together, and drizzle with olive oil before serving.

Grilled Antipasto Skewers

Servings: 5

Ingredients

2 tbsp. olive oil
Pinch of salt
1 tsp. Italian herbs
1 small eggplant, cut into 1-inch cubes
1 small zucchini, cut into 1-inch cubes
1 medium red bell pepper, cut into 1-inch squares
1 cup 1-inch cheese cubes

Instructions

1. Place cast-iron grill pan over medium heat. Brush with olive oil.
2. Season vegetables with salt and dried herbs. Grill for 7–10 minutes or until softened.
3. Skewer vegetables and cheese. Serve warm.

Fruit Skewers with Peanut Butter Cream

Servings: 6

Ingredients

3 oz. strawberries
1 kiwi, cut into 1-inch cubes
1 banana, cut into ½-inch rounds
1 pear, cut into 1-inch cubes
2 tbsp. smooth peanut butter
2 tbsp. cream cheese
1 tbsp. maple syrup
1 tbsp. water
1 tbsp. shredded coconut

Instructions

1. Skewer fruits and berries together as desired.
2. Whisk peanut butter with cream cheese and maple syrup, adding the water as needed.
3. Top skewers with cream and sprinkle with shredded coconut.

Cherry Chocolate Cookie Sandwiches

Servings: 5

Ingredients

1½ cups gluten-free flour of choice
$^1/_3$ cup cocoa powder
$^2/_3$ tsp baking powder
Pinch of salt
$^2/_3$ cup sugar
¼ cup milk of choice
½ cup vegetable oil
3 oz. cream cheese
½ tsp. vanilla extract
¼ cup canned cherries, chopped

Instructions

1. Preheat oven to 350°F.
2. Combine flour, cocoa, baking powder, and salt.
3. In another bowl, whisk together sugar, milk, and vegetable oil until pale.
4. Combine wet and dry ingredients to form a dough. Roll the dough into 10 balls and place on a parchment-covered baking sheet.
5. Bake for 10–12 minutes and let cool completely.
6. Combine cream cheese, vanilla, and cherries. Sandwich cherry cream between two cookies.

Chewy Coconut Ice Cream Sandwiches

Servings: 4

Ingredients

½ cup vegetable oil
½ cup coconut milk
1 cup shredded coconut
1 cup gluten-free flour of choice
1 cup coconut sugar
1 tsp. baking powder
4–6 scoops your favorite non-dairy ice cream

Instructions

1. Preheat your oven to 375°F.
2. Combine vegetable oil and milk.
3. Mix together the coconut, flour, sugar, and baking powder. Add wet ingredients to the dry ingredients and mix until uniform dough forms.
4. Make 8 cookies.
5. Bake for 18–20 minutes and leave to cool completely.
6. Sandwich each ice cream scoop between two cookies and serve immediately.

Peanut Butter Banana Bites

Servings: 10

Ingredients

1 large banana, sliced into 20 rounds
5 tsp. smooth peanut butter
½ cup dark chocolate, chopped
Pinch of sea salt

Instructions

1. Fill a pot about a quarter full with water and heat to simmer. Place a heat-proof bowl with chopped chocolate on top of it and stir the chocolate until it melts (or use your double boiler if you have one).
2. Top 10 banana rounds with peanut butter. Cover with leftover banana.
3. Dip half of each sandwich into melted chocolate and place on a sheet of parchment paper. Season with a tiny pinch of salt.
4. Serve after chocolate hardens.

Strawberry Chocolate "Shots"

Servings: 8

Ingredients

½ pound strawberries
2/3 cup dark chocolate, chopped
2 tbsp. coconut cream (from the top of a can of coconut milk)

Instructions

1. With a small teaspoon, remove the insides of each strawberry (about halfway) to make a cup.
2. Melt chopped chocolate over double boiler (or see previous recipe if you don't have one!). Slightly cut the pointy end of each strawberry and dip it in chocolate. Place berries on parchment to set, chocolate end down. When the chocolate sets, you'll have sturdy strawberry cup.
3. Re-melt leftover chocolate over double boiler. Add coconut cream while mixing constantly to make a smooth ganache.
4. Fill each strawberry cup with ganache.

Strawberry Cups with White Chocolate Cream

Servings: 8–10

Ingredients

8–10 strawberries, stems removed
½ cup cream cheese, room temperature
3 tbsp. white chocolate, melted
¼ tsp. vanilla extract

Instructions

1. With a small teaspoon, scoop out the insides of each strawberry.
2. Whisk white chocolate into cream cheese. Add vanilla extract.
3. Fill each strawberry with white chocolate cream and let it chill before serving.

Raw Cookie Sandwiches with Date Caramel

Servings: 3

Ingredients

For the cookies:
1 cup oat flour
¼ cup maple syrup
½ tsp. cinnamon
4 large Medjool dates, pitted and pureed

For the caramel:
1 cup large Medjool dates, pitted
1 tbsp. maple syrup
1 tbsp. peanut butter
½ tsp. vanilla extract

Instructions

1. Mix all cookie ingredients until you create a sticky, uniform dough.
2. Wet your hands and make 6 round cookies. Place each over parchment and keep in freezer while making caramel.
3. For the caramel, puree the dates with syrup and peanut butter. Season with just a bit of vanilla.
4. Sandwich the caramel between two cookies before serving.

Double Chocolate Cookie Sandwiches

Servings: 4

Ingredients

1 cup oat flour
8 large Medjool dates (about 1 cup), pitted and pureed
2 tbsp. cacao powder
1 tbsp. avocado oil
2 tbsp. maple syrup
Pinch of salt
2 tbsp. vegan chocolate spread

Instructions

1. Mix first five ingredients together. Season with a small pinch of sea salt.
2. Make eight cookies. Freeze to set (about 2–3 hours).
3. Sandwich ½ tablespoon of your favorite chocolate spread between two cookies and serve.

Stuffed Peaches with Vanilla Ice Cream

Servings: 3

Ingredients

3 tsp. brown sugar
½ tsp. cinnamon
3 peaches
3 tbsp. premade granola
3 small scoops of your favorite vanilla ice cream

Instructions

1. Preheat your oven to 400°F. Mix the brown sugar and cinnamon together.
2. Cut each peach in half and remove the pit. Sprinkle each sliced peach with sugar-cinnamon mixture and bake for 10–12 minutes or until soft and caramelized.
3. Spoon granola onto 3 peach halves and place a scoop of ice cream on top. Top with leftover peach halves.

Grilled Peach Cups

Servings: 4

Ingredients

2 peaches
1 tsp. melted butter
1 tbsp. honey
½ cup cream cheese
2 tbsp. heavy cream
½ tsp. vanilla extract

Instructions

1. Cut each peach in half and remove pits.
2. Whisk melted butter with honey and brush the mixture over the peaches.
3. Heat your grill over the medium heat and place peaches on it cut side down. Grill for 2 minutes or until brown marks appear.
4. Whisk cream cheese with heavy cream and vanilla. Top each peach half with cream before serving.

Cottage Cheese Pancake Tacos with Berry Compote

Servings: 4

Ingredients

2 cups cottage cheese
1 egg
¼ cup brown sugar
½ cup gluten-free flour of choice
½ tsp. baking powder
2 tbsp. vegetable oil
1 cup mixed berries
¼ cup white sugar

Instructions

1. Combine cottage cheese with egg, brown sugar, flour, and baking powder. Divide and shape the mixture into 4 pancake shapes.
2. Heat vegetable oil and fry 4 patties for 2 minutes on each side.
3. For the berry compote, mash barriers with sugar and place over low heat for 3–4 minutes, stirring occasionally. Add a couple tablespoons of water if berries get stuck to the bottom of the pan.
4. Right before eating, place some compote over the pancake and fold in half to make a "taco shell."

Conversion Charts

METRIC AND IMPERIAL CONVERSIONS
(These conversions are rounded for convenience)

Ingredient	Cups/Tablespoons/ Teaspoons	Ounces	Grams/Milliliters
Butter	1 cup = 16 tablespoons = 2 sticks	8 ounces	230 grams
Cheese, shredded	1 cup	4 ounces	110 grams
Cream cheese	1 tablespoon	0.5 ounce	14.5 grams
Cornstarch	1 tablespoon	0.3 ounce	8 grams
Flour, all-purpose	1 cup/1 tablespoon	4.5 ounces/0.3 ounce	125 grams/8 grams
Flour, whole wheat	1 cup	4 ounces	120 grams
Fruit, dried	1 cup	4 ounces	120 grams
Fruits or veggies, chopped	1 cup	5 to 7 ounces	145 to 200 grams
Fruits or veggies, puréed	1 cup	8.5 ounces	245 grams
Honey, maple syrup, or corn syrup	1 tablespoon	0.75 ounce	20 grams
Liquids: cream, milk, water, or juice	1 cup	8 fluid ounces	240 milliliters
Oats	1 cup	5.5 ounces	150 grams
Salt	1 teaspoon	0.2 ounce	6 grams
Spices: cinnamon, cloves, ginger, or nutmeg (ground)	1 teaspoon	0.2 ounce	5 milliliters
Sugar, brown, firmly packed	1 cup	7 ounces	200 grams
Sugar, white	1 cup/1 tablespoon	7 ounces/0.5 ounce	200 grams/12.5 grams
Vanilla extract	1 teaspoon	0.2 ounce	4 grams

OVEN TEMPERATURES

Fahrenheit	Celsius	Gas Mark
225°	110°	¼
250°	120°	½
275°	140°	1
300°	150°	2
325°	160°	3
350°	180°	4
375°	190°	5
400°	200°	6
425°	220°	7
450°	230°	8